Plants All Around

Plants live almost everywhere. They grow in places that are very cold, very hot, dry or wet. Some plants lose their **leaves** every year, some keep them. There are lots of plants we can eat!

Many people like to have plants in their gardens and homes. We can also see plants in parks and growing in the countryside.

The many plants in one of the National Parks of Sri Lanka.

📖 1 **What do you already know about plants?**

📖 2 **Draw a plant and label the parts you know.**

In this book we will learn a lot about plants and how they live. We will learn that they are similar, whether they live in hot, cold, wet, or dry areas, and how they can be different from each other.

T0385922

Plants are Alive

Plants are living things. They change and grow. Even though they are alive, plants are not the same as animals.

Look at the pictures below. Some of these things are living, some are not.

1 List the living things.

2a Which of the living things are plants?

2b How do you know they are plants?

Here are some living and non-living things: bird, flower, lamp, tree, oryx, grass.

Flowering plants, grass and trees are all different types of plants.

Describing Plants

Plants grow where they can get air, light and water.

There are lots of plants all over the world. Plants can be tall, short or spiky. Some plants can climb walls and there are even a few that eat insects!

How a plant grows.

This spiky plant is called a cactus.

This climbing plant is called a Mexican flame vine.

📖 **1 With a partner make a list of words to describe plants.**

Parts of Plants

All plants have the same parts, but they may look very different from one type of plant to another.

This plant has four parts.

Each part has a different name.

Each part has a different job to do.

1 Which part is the **flower**? Point to it.

2a Do all plants have flowers?

2b Explain your answer.

4

Science Skills

Leaves – Observe it!

When you look at the plants around where you live you will see that each type of plant has a different sort of leaf.

Leaves have different shapes, sizes and textures. Some are shiny, some are dull. Some are smooth and some are hairy. Leaves help us to identify a plant.

Bougainvillea

Date palm

Geranium leaves

How many different leaves can you find? Find leaves that are tiny, spiky, rounded, smooth, large, pointed, rough, two-colours, shiny or dark.

1 Describe two different leaves you have found. How are they different?

2 Find out the names of the plants they come from.

3 Look at your leaves with a magnifying glass. What can you see?

Growing Plants

Grow your own plant

You will need ... **compost**, small plants, plant pot, water

1 Put some compost into a plant pot.

2 Carefully put your plant into the compost. Make sure the roots are covered.

3 Give the plant some water.

4 Look closely at your plant every few days and water it when the compost is dry.

5 Record what happens to your plant by drawing pictures or taking photos.

6 Add these to a classroom display.

Grow your own plant!

Collect plants from your local area or from your garden (make sure you have permission). Look at them closely.

1 How is each plant the same?

2 How are they different?

Trees are Plants Too!

Do trees have the same parts as plants? The answer is yes. Trees are plants too. Trees are large tall plants with thick woody stems.

The stem of a tree is called the **trunk**. The outside part of the trunk is called the **bark**. Bark can be very rough.

Word box
bark
trunk

Acacia tree

1 Name the parts of this tree?

Local plants and trees

You will need ...

pens, pencils, colouring pencils, erasers, paper

1 Find a small flowering plant and a large tree where you live. Draw them and find out their names.

2 Do the two plants have the same parts? Label your drawings.

Deciduous Trees

1 Look at the two pictures of this tree. What happened to the tree in winter?

Word box
branches
deciduous
twigs

This is an English oak tree in summer.

This is the same tree in winter.

In some countries, some trees lose their leaves during colder times of the year. When the leaves fall off you can see the **branches** and **twigs**. In hot countries some trees lose their leaves in the dry season. Trees that lose their leaves are called **deciduous** trees. They are still alive even when they do not have any leaves.

Evergreen Trees

Ghaf tree

Word box

evergreen

1 Look at the two evergreen trees.

1a How do they look the same?

1b How do they look different?

This ghaf tree has leaves all through the year. Trees that keep their leaves all year are called **evergreen** trees.

Evergreen trees are found all over the world.

These are pine trees. Pine trees have very thin, spiky leaves called pine needles.

Find out about one deciduous and one evergreen tree that grow where you live.

More About Trees

This is a date palm tree. The leaves are known as fronds.

1 Name the parts of this tree. Point to the trunk, branches, leaves and fruit of the tree.

Word box
blossom
fruit

This is a Flame tree.

Look closely.

Some trees have flowers that we call **blossom.** There are seed pods on this tree too.

2 Does this tree have the same parts as a date palm tree? Explain your answer.

You will need ... paper, crayons, a tree

1 Take rubbings of the bark and leaves of some different trees in your area using crayons.

Plants and Their Parts

From flowering plants ...

Zinnia

... to bushes ...

Tropical hibiscus

... to trees ...

Frangipani tree

... most plants have the same main parts:

flowers, stems (or trunk), leaves and roots.

📖 **1 What other words do you know for plant parts?**

Plants we Eat

Plants are healthy food for humans. We enjoy eating them and they can taste delicious.

We eat different parts of plants.

Carrots, cabbage and parsley.

We eat roots such as carrots.

We eat the leaves of plants such as cabbage and lettuce.

We eat the stems of plants such as parsley.

Tomatoes, apples and papaya are all fruits from plants that we eat.

1 Think of another plant stem that we eat.

Papaya

What plants have you eaten?

1 List the plants you have eaten today.
2 Which parts of the plants (stem, root, leaves or fruits) did you eat?

2a Does your family grow plants to eat?
2b If yes, which ones?

Science Skills

Observe it!

Observing means looking very closely at things. We can use all our senses to discover more.

Be careful – never taste plants you do not know. Some plants are **poisonous** and can make us ill.

investigating different fruits

Wash your hands first.

in groups:

1 Feel the different fruits and describe how they feel.

2 Look at them and describe their shape and colour.

3 Cut the fruit in half with a plastic knife (ask an adult to help).

4 What can you see inside the fruits? Use a magnifying glass.

5 Smell and taste the fruits. Describe how they taste.

Make an Herbarium

An herbarium is a collection of dried plants. Scientists use them to help name plants they do not know.

Dried plants

You will need ... sheet of card, thick paper, plant, pen or pencil, glue, newspapers, heavy books

1 Place the plant between two sheets of newspaper. Put some heavy books on top.

2 Leave for a week.

3 Remove your plant and glue it to the paper.

4 Add the name of your plant and where you found it.

5 Label the parts of the plant.

6 Stick your completed herbarium to the card.

Making a Model of a Plant

Here is a model of plants that Class I have made.

1 Point to the flower, stem and leaves.

You will need... paper, cardboard, glue, pencils, crayons, other junk and arts and crafts materials as available

1 Use your materials to make a model of a plant.

2 Label the flower, stem, leaves and roots on your model then display it.

3 Write instructions to help someone else to make your plant.

Glossary

Bark outer layer of the trunk

Blossom a flower or mass of flowers on a tree or bush

Branch part of a tree that grows from the trunk

Compost a type of soil used to grow plants

Deciduous a tree that loses its leaves at certain times of year

Evergreen a tree that has leaves throughout the year

Flower the part of a plant that is usually brightly coloured

Fruit the sweet, juicy part of the plant, for example, orange and papaya

Leaf/leaves the flat, green part of a plant that grows from the stem

Poisonous can harm us if eaten; make us ill

Trunk thick, woody stem of a tree

Twig a small woody shoot growing from a branch